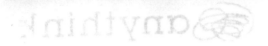

MINI ANIMALS

Mini Pigs

by Alix Wood

WINDMILL
BOOKS

New York

Published in 2017 by **Windmill Books**, An Imprint of Rosen Publishing
29 East 21st Street, New York, NY 10010

Editor: Eloise Macgregor
Designer: Alix Wood
Consultant: Stephanie Matlock, Vice President of the American Mini Pig Association

Cover, 1 © www.petpiggies.co.uk; 4, 5, 6, 7, 8, 9, 12, 15, 16, 17, 19 bottom, 20, 21 bottom, 22, 24, 29 © Adobe Stock; 10 © Joshua Lutz; 11 © Shutterstock; 13 © Purdy Petite Piggies; 14 © Nancy K. Hicks; 18 © Dsmoran/Dreamstime; 19 top © iStock; 21 top © Henry Williams; 23 © Jules Baldwin-Cooper; 25 © Angelo Jacques/Saartje Venmans; 26 © Malisa Schulz James; 27 © mattyc1965/123RF Stock Photo; 28 © Michelle Ross Dietz/Jyll Latham

Cataloging-in-Publication Data
Names: Wood, Alix.
Title: Mini pigs / Alix Wood.
Description: New York : Windmill Books, 2017. | Series: Mini animals| Includes index.
Identifiers: ISBN 9781499481556 (pbk.) | ISBN 9781499481563 (library bound) |
   ISBN 9781508192961 (6 pack)
Subjects: LCSH: Swine--Juvenile literature.
Classification: LCC SF395.5 W66 2017 | DDC 636.4'0887--dc23

Manufactured in the United States of America
CPSIA Compliance Information: Batch #: BW17PK. For Further Information contact: Windmill Books, New York, New York at 1-866-478-0556

Contents

Cute Little Pigs

A miniature pig, or mini pig, is a very small pig. They are sometimes known as teacup pigs, because their **piglets** are small enough to fit in a teacup.

A fully grown mini pig weighs between 75 pounds (34 kg) and 150 pounds (68 kg). That's around the size of a very large dog. Even though mini pigs are smaller than normal pigs, they certainly wouldn't fit in a teacup as adults!

Cute Alert!

This newborn piglet could fit in the palm of your hand.

Pigs are **sociable** animals. They will get lonely if they are kept on their own. They are best kept with other pigs. They don't always get along with other animals.

Why A.e the Pigs So Cmall?

In the 1960s, small pigs were bred specially for use in medical **research**. Medically, pigs are similar to humans in many ways and make useful research animals. The smaller pigs were easier to handle and needed less room. These small pigs became popular in petting zoos, too. People loved them and began to want mini pigs as pets.

Cute Alert!
This Saint Bernard puppy and his mini pig friend will grow to be around the same size.

It takes time to create a smaller pig. **Breeders** gradually developed mini pigs by choosing their smallest pigs to have piglets. Then they selected the smallest of these piglets to have more piglets. Over time, each **generation** of pigs got smaller.

Mini pigs are not all one breed. There are over 50 different types of mini pig. The smallest natural breed of domestic pig is the kunekune. Many mini pigs have been bred from kunekune pigs.

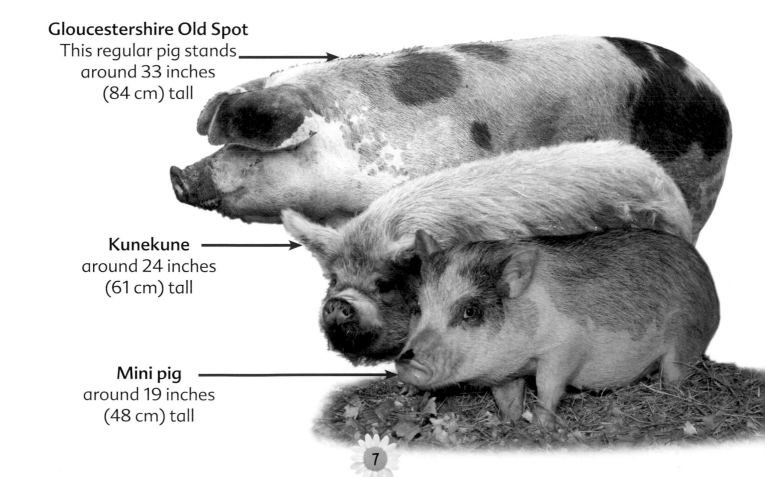

Gloucestershire Old Spot
This regular pig stands around 33 inches (84 cm) tall

Kunekune
around 24 inches (61 cm) tall

Mini pig
around 19 inches (48 cm) tall

Kunekune Pigs

Kunekunes come from New Zealand. They are hairy, stocky pigs with short legs. They are very intelligent. With patience, they can be taught the same commands that a dog understands.

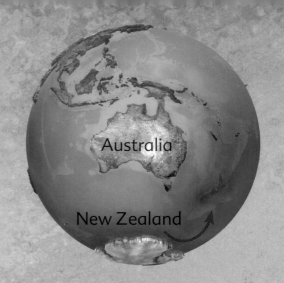

Australia

New Zealand

Kunekunes are **placid**, friendly, and love human company. They are popular with pig owners. They mainly eat grass. Their upturned noses cause less damage to the ground when they **root** than other pigs' noses do.

tassel

Many kunekunes have two fleshy tassels, known as "piri piri," under their chins.

In the late 1970s there were only about 50 kunekunes left in New Zealand. Wildlife park owners Michael Willis and John Simister started a breeding program. Their work saved the breed from extinction.

Potbellied Pigs

Potbellied pigs originally came from Asia, mainly from Vietnam. An adult's belly will often nearly touch the ground! It's important not to overfeed this breed of pig. Like most pigs, potbellies have poor eyesight. They make up for this with excellent hearing and sense of smell.

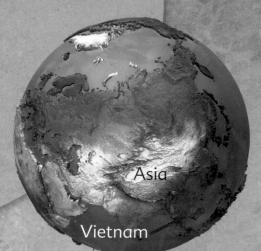

Asia

Vietnam

Cute Alert!
You can tell how potbellied pigs got their name!

Potbellied pigs love to be scratched and massaged, and enjoy a tummy rub. Like most pigs, they do not like to be picked up. This frightens them and they may squeal very loudly! Potbellies will happily cuddle up next to their human owners, though.

Potbellies have little hair on their bodies. They need plenty of shade to protect their skin from the sun. They also need some mud to **wallow** in. The mud protects and soothes their skin.

American Mini Pigs

Most mini pigs in America are a mixture of several breeds. Back in the 1940s, breeders developed the Minnesota mini pig from Guinea hogs, wild boars, and a small wild hog from Louisiana known as the piney wood rooter.

Recently, Minnesota mini pigs have been crossed with other breeds, including potbellies and a German mini breed, the Göttingen (right).

The Göttingen itself is the result of crossbreeding Minnesota mini pigs, Vietnamese potbelly pigs, and German Landrace pigs.

Cute Alert!
You can see the Göttingen are full of personality!

12

The American Mini Pig is now a recognized breed itself. With so many different breeds all mixed together, American Mini Pigs can be spotted or striped, black, or ginger, and practically all the shapes and colors in between!

To be sure how large an American Mini Pig will grow, it is essential to meet the parents. Their piglets usually grow to around the same size.

Mini Pigs as Pets

Mini pigs have become popular pets. Some owners even bring their pigs indoors. Pigs are naturally clean so it is easy to train them to use a cat **litter box**. Mini pigs are covered in hair, not fur, so they do not shed. They live for around 15 years, so deciding to get a pig is a long-term **commitment**.

Cute Alert!

Some mini pig owners are happy to let their pigs sleep in their beds. Other house pigs sleep in a dog bed or crate.

Mini pigs need outside space, too. Pigs are perfectly happy living outside, but they do need a warm, dry shelter and some company.

There are several things you need to consider before you get a pet mini pig. Check if your local area allows pigs as pets. In some areas it is illegal to keep pigs as they are considered to be farm animals.

When buying a pig, be wary, as mini pigs can grow much bigger than their breeders claim. Some dishonest breeders have been known to starve their pigs to keep them small. Check the size and age of the piglet's parents. Mini pigs aren't full grown until they are 5 years old.

Caring for a Mini Pig

Mini pigs are not the easiest pet to keep. They need the usual things many animals require, such as fresh water daily, the right amount of food, and somewhere warm and dry to sleep.

Mini pigs have some special requirements, too. Pigs will eat just about anything, so their diet and exercise regimen is very important so they don't get overweight. Many mini pigs suffer from sunburn. Shelter from the sun and mud baths are essential in the warmer months!

Pale pigs burn on sunny days. They welcome some sunscreen!

Cute Alert!

Pigs don't really smell, but they do enjoy bath time if introduced to the idea gently. Pigs have dry skin, so use a moisturizing shampoo.

Pigs need a safe, warm place to sleep

A Mini Pig Care Checklist

These are some of the things that a mini pig needs:

1. Fresh water

2. Suitable food such as grazing or special pig feed. Pigs should not be fed kitchen waste.

3. Warm, dry shelter and outside space with shade

4. Regular veterinary checkups

5. Plenty of company

6. A few treats such as raisins, fresh fruit, and vegetables

7. Toys to relieve boredom

Mini Piglets

Female pigs are called **sows**. Like other pig breeds, miniature sows carry their young for around three months, three weeks, and three days. They usually have about six piglets, but can have as many as twelve! Mini pigs are **mammals**. Mammals' young drink milk produced by their mother.

Cute Alert!

These piglets are drinking milk through teats on their mother's tummy. Each piglet always suckles from the same teat.

Newborn piglets need to be kept warm. In nature they would all snuggle together next to their mother for warmth. Sometimes a mother may roll on top of her piglets and hurt them. Instead, to keep them warm, owners may put the piglets under a heat lamp (right) or wrap them in blankets.

Little piglets love to play outside on a warm day. Some owners put them inside a child's playpen to keep them safe while they enjoy the outdoors.

Clever Little Pigs

Miniature pigs are very intelligent. Pigs are believed to be the fourth smartest species on Earth. Only humans, chimpanzees, and dolphins are smarter. Pigs have good memories and are great problem solvers.

Just like a dog, pigs can recognize their own name and obey spoken commands. They have a great sense of direction, and can find their way home over long distances. Pigs learn from watching each other and from watching us.

Cute Alert!

Pigs have been tested and found to be smarter than the average four-year-old child!

Toys such as balls help keep mini pigs from getting bored. It needs to be a sturdy ball, though. They often bite them and make them burst!

Some owners give their pigs baby toys to play with. Pigs really enjoy playing baby pianos, or pressing the buttons on pop-up toys! Owners must make sure the toys are strong enough to not break if they are bitten or stepped on. Sharp plastic could hurt a pig.

Amazing Noses

Pigs have poor eyesight. Their sensitive **snouts** help them find their way around. Pig snouts are specially developed for rooting in the ground to search for food. Pigs communicate using their snouts. They can easily recognize each other by their scent.

Pigs are able to smell odors around 25 feet (7.6 m) under the ground! Because of this amazing ability, farmers have used them for centuries to sniff out **truffles**, an expensive food that grows underground.

Many farmers switched to using sniffer dogs instead, though, as the pigs would eat too many of the truffles!

Cute Alert!

Pigs greet each other using their snouts. Two pigs will sometimes sleep nose-to-nose, too!

A pig's nose is around 2,000 times more sensitive than a human nose. It is perfectly shaped for rooting around in the mud for food, too.

23

Working Mini Pigs

Because of their amazing sense of smell, mini pigs are sometimes used by law enforcers to sniff for illegal goods. The pigs learn fast. They are cheaper to feed than dogs, and usually live longer. Their ability to smell buried objects makes them useful like dogs, too. The only drawback is they can't climb around vehicles or baggage as well.

Mini pigs are used by the military to sniff out **land mines**, too. Land mines are dangerous explosives that are usually buried under the soil.

As rooting around in the mud is part of a pig's natural behavior, they really enjoy their work.

Mini pigs are great at helping farmers or gardeners plow their land. While the pigs are **foraging** for roots and food beneath the ground, they push their strong snouts deep into the soil. This plows the soil, and the pigs eat all the weeds. They **fertilize** the soil with manure, too!

Cute Alert!

Mini pigs' cute flat snouts are perfect for digging. The round disk at the tip is connected to strong muscles that help it move through the ground.

At the Showground

Part of the fun of keeping farm animals is entering them in agricultural shows. If you have a **pedigree** pig, they can compete for the "best in breed." Young owners can enter young stock handler competitions, too.

Before a show, it's important to get a pig used to being handled. Pigs are usually expected to walk free in the ring, with no lead or harness. They are guided using gentle taps with a cane. This takes some practice!

Cute Alert!

No matter how well you train, your pig may just be in a difficult mood on the day!

In a young stock handler class the judge may expect the handler to know the breed, age, weight, and sex of the pig.

Pigs are soaped and scrubbed before a show. They need a good rinse as their dry skin means they can get dandruff! It's important that the owners look neat and presentable too.

Some owners trim the hair around a pig's ears. They rub baby oil on the pig, too, to make its coat shine. Pale pigs are sometimes dusted with talcum powder. Just before entering the ring the pigs get a final brush and hoof cleaning.

This mini pig has won some prizes.

Test Your Knowledge

1. Which situation makes a mini pig happiest?
   a) being alone
   b) being with other pigs
   c) being with other animals

2. Where do kunekune pigs come from?
   a) Wisconsin
   b) Europe
   c) New Zealand

3. What is a female pig called?
   a) a sow b) a cow
   c) a piglet

4. Can pigs' noses smell things buried underground?
   a) no b) yes

5   Why do mini pigs like to cover themselves in mud?
    a) They just love mud
    b) It keeps them from getting sunburned
    c) They're naughty

6   How long do sows carry their young?
    a) two months
    b) three years
    c) three months, three weeks, and three days

7   Would an adult mini pig fit in a teacup?
    a) yes b) no

8   Why would you give a pig a ball?
    a) no reason
    b) to play with
    c) you shouldn't give a pig a ball

How did you do? The answers are on page 32.

Glossary

breeders People who raise animals to produce the animals' young.

commitment A promise to do something.

fertilize Make soil better by adding animal dung or chemicals.

foraging Searching for food or supplies.

generation A group of individuals born and living at the same time.

land mines Explosives laid on or just under the ground.

litter box A tray designed for indoor animals to go to the bathroom in.

mammals Warm-blooded animals that have a backbone and hair, breathe air, and feed milk to their young.

pedigree A pure breed with recorded parentage.

piglets Baby pigs.

placid Peaceful and calm.

research Careful study and investigation to discover and explain new knowledge.

root To burrow in or dig up the earth in search of food, using the snout.

snouts Pigs' noses.

sociable Likely to seek or enjoy companionship.

sows Adult female hogs.

truffle An edible fungus that grows underground.

wallow To roll about in deep mud.

Further Information

Books

Lunis, Natalie. *Potbellied Pigs (Peculiar Pets)*. New York, NY: Bearport Publishing, 2009.

Orr, Tamra. *How To Convince Your Parents You Can Care for a Potbellied Pig (Robbie Readers)*. Hockessin, DE: Mitchell Lane Publishers, 2008.

Reed, Christie. *Mini Pig (You Have a Pet What?!)*. Vero Beach, FL: Rourke Educational Media, 2015.

Websites

For web resources related to the subject of this book, go to: **www.windmillbooks.com/weblinks** and select this book's title.

Index

Answers 1) b, 2) c, 3) a, 4) b, 5) b, 6) c, 7) b, 8) b